BE STILL

Bible Words of Peace and Comfort

by

Chris Wright

First published in the USA by Lighthouse Christian Publishing ©Chris Wright 2009

Paperback ISBN: 978-0-9932760-7-1
e-Book ISBN: 978-0-9933941-4-0

PUBLISHED BY
WHITE TREE PUBLISHING
BRISTOL
UNITED KINGDOM

wtpbristol@gmail.com

Introduction

The Bible contains wonderful promises of love and forgiveness for those who turn to God, and frequent words of warning for those who reject him. Although it would be dangerous to ignore the words of warning, there may come a time in our lives when we want to concentrate on God's many promises of peace and comfort. The readings in this book are for people, young or old, who want to know what it means to be held securely in the Lord's comforting arms.

The pages are shared by two separate months. So January and July share the same readings, as do February and August, March and September, April and October, May and November, and June and December. There are also special readings for Easter and Christmas. Start on today's date, and you can keep going until you come back to where you started – six months later! There is, of course, no reason why you should not keep going if you're finding it helpful.

You need to find the Bible verses yourself, and this allows you to use your favourite version. This will be particularly welcomed by older readers who may want to read or hear words that are familiar.

The readings can be started on any day of the year, but after six months you will be repeating your original reading, question and prayer. There is no reason why you should not keep going for as many months or years as you want, as long as you find it helpful. However, this book is not intended to take the place of personal Bible reading, study and prayer.

Here are a few suggestions for going deeper. (There are, of course, many other sources than these.) Visit *www.ewordtoday.com* for free online Bible reading plans, in several languages, including *The Bible in One Year* with 365 readings arranged in chronological order starting on any date you choose. Reading plans are on *www.biblegateway.com.* See also *www.youversion.com* for hundreds of free Bible versions in many languages online. *www.cwr.org.uk* and *www.scriptureunion.org.uk* are just two publishers of daily Bible-reading notes and other useful study material.

You will also benefit from a Bible commentary -- expensive, but probably a lot cheaper than your phone, tablet or sports kit! If you need help in choosing the most appropriate reading material for yourself, ask your church leader or a Christian bookshop for advice.

As well as being for personal use, these readings are intended for sharing with anyone in special need, to help them draw comfort from the Bible reading and prayer for that date. If these pages raise important questions, discuss them with your pastor or a close Christian friend. Bible reading and prayer are the two most important ways of getting to know and trust Jesus Christ, our Lord and Saviour.

You have the find the Bible verses yourself, and this allows you to use your favourite version. This will be particularly welcomed by older readers who may want to read or hear words that are familiar.

As well as being for personal use, these readings are intended for sharing with anyone in special need, to help them draw comfort from the Bible reading and the prayer for that date. If these pages raise important questions, discuss them with your pastor or a close Christian friend. Bible reading and prayer are the two most important ways of getting to know and trust Jesus Christ, our Lord and Saviour.

JANUARY 1
JULY 1

QUESTION: Do you think you found Jesus all by yourself, or can you now see that he came looking for you – because he loves you?

Luke 15:8-10

PRAYER: Thank you, Jesus, that you love me so much that even though you have plenty of other followers, you took the time to come looking for me.

* * * *

JANUARY 2
JULY 2

QUESTION: How do we know that the things we read in the Bible are reliable? Well, here's one reason. It contains the accounts of eyewitnesses – people who were there at the time. An example of this is Luke's account of the life of Jesus. He interviewed people who knew Jesus.

Luke 1:1-4

PRAYER: Thank you, Jesus, that people who were there at the time, people who walked and talked with you, wrote down so many things about you.

JANUARY 3
JULY 3

QUESTION: "In that day" is a prophecy to the coming of Jesus 700 years after these verses were written. So can you say today that God is your salvation, and you will trust and not be afraid?

Isaiah 12:1-6

PRAYER: Thank you, Lord, that you are my salvation. Help me trust you and not be afraid.

* * * *

JANUARY 4
JULY 4

QUESTION: Peter knows who Jesus is. How do you think he knew? Are there things that you know, things that were hidden to you before you became a Christian? Think about it.

Matthew 16:13-17

PRAYER: Heavenly Father, thank you for showing me many things about yourself in the Bible – things that were once hidden to me. Thank you above all for... (Can you think of something special to include here?)

JANUARY 5
JULY 5

QUESTION: Have you ever heard of “Living Water”? What do you think it is? Have you drunk any of it yet?

John 4:4-14

PRAYER: Lord Jesus, help me never to be thirsty again, but to really understand what this Living Water is, and drink it today and for ever.

* * * *

JANUARY 6
JULY 6

QUESTION: This prophecy is looking much further ahead than to the time of Jesus. When do you think it will be fulfilled?

Isaiah 25:6-9

PRAYER SUGGESTION: Use the last three lines of today’s reading in a time of praise, but change “our”, “we” and “us” to “my”, “I” “me”.

JANUARY 7
JULY 7

QUESTION: Do you think Jesus will only accept you if you're "good enough"? Are you one of the (self) righteous – or are you a sinner? Read who Jesus preferred.

Mark 2:13-17

PRAYER: Please forgive me, Lord, when I think I have to be "good enough" for you to want me. I thank you that even though I am a sinner, you love me.

* * * *

JANUARY 8
JULY 8

QUESTION: Why do you think some seed doesn't grow properly after it's sown? Do you know people who have heard the gospel and lost interest? Has it ever happened to you?

Luke 8:4-8
Continued tomorrow

PRAYER SUGGESTION: Think of someone you know who seemed to have started well in the Christian life, but has now lost interest. Pray that they will regain their faith. If it's you, pray that you will regain the faith you once had.

JANUARY 9
JULY 9

Continued from yesterday
QUESTION: Think back to when you first thought seriously about Jesus and his claims. Were you like the good soil in this parable, or like the other ground? What sort of ground are you now?

Luke 8:11-15

PRAYER: Lord Jesus, sometimes the thorns grow up, and the seed that you planted in my life doesn't seem to grow properly. Sometimes it doesn't get watered. Please make me like the good soil in this parable, and be useful to you.

* * * *

JANUARY 10
JULY 10

QUESTION: Do you think God ever gets tired? No? So why do we sometimes think he's too tired to bother with us?

Isaiah 40:25-31

PRAYER: Lord, please give me strength in my soul to soar on wings like an eagle, to run and not grow weary, to walk and not be faint.

JANUARY 11
JULY 11

QUESTION: You don't have to be a theologian to become a Christian. Maybe it even helps if you're not! Did you find it easy to become a child of God?

Mark 10:13-16

PRAYER: Lord God, there are so many things I do not understand about you. When life is dark and puzzling, please help me just to trust you, like a child who trusts a loving parent.

* * * *

JANUARY 12
JULY 12

QUESTION: Jesus says that this account of the woman who gave everything to him will be told around the world. Well, here it is! What would you have done if you were this woman, without knowing what Jesus was about to say about you?

Matthew 26:6-13

PRAYER SUGGESTION: Tell Jesus what you would like to do for him, if only you could. And then think if there's any way you can do it. Of course, he may have something else in mind for you! Pray about it.

JANUARY 13
JULY 13

QUESTION: Paul is writing to the young church in Philippi, reminding them that he has shown them how a Christian should live. Is your mind always on earthly things, or do you believe your citizenship is in heaven?

Philippians 3:17-21

PRAYER SUGGESTION: Tell Jesus just how much you're looking forward to his return to take you to heaven, to be with him for ever.

* * * *

JANUARY 14
JULY 14

QUESTION: Do you know that the Lord is forgiving and good, abounding in love to all who call to him? Well, he is!

Psalm 86:1-7
Continued tomorrow

PRAYER FROM TODAY'S READING: Please, Lord, bring joy to me, your child and your servant – for to you, O Lord, I lift up my soul.

JANUARY 15
JULY 15

Continued from yesterday
QUESTION: A big problem in life is that we have all sorts of gods today, but can you say with the Psalmist that there is only one God for you?

Psalm 86:8-13

PRAYER FROM TODAY'S READING: "Teach me your way, O Lord, and I will walk in your truth; give me an undivided heart, that I may fear your name. I will praise you, O Lord my God, with all my heart; I will glorify your name for ever."

* * * *

JANUARY 16
JULY 16

QUESTION: The worst storms in life are usually those that strike without warning. Can you sympathize with the disciples of Jesus in this story?

Mark 4:35-41

PRAYER: Thank you, Jesus, that even when troubles come without warning, you are there with me. Please help me trust you more.

JANUARY 17
JULY 17

QUESTION: How often do you praise God? Every day? Only when you remember? Have you ever told anyone else about God, so his name can be passed down from generation to generation?

Psalm 145:1-8

PRAYER: Lord God, help me understand that you are gracious and compassionate, slow to anger and rich in love. And help me tell other people about you.

* * * *

JANUARY 18
JULY 18

QUESTION: Do you find it amazing that we have the words of a prayer that Jesus actually taught?

Matthew 6:9-18

PRAYER SUGGESTION: Pray the Lord's Prayer – and mean all of it.

JANUARY 19
JULY 19

QUESTION: Jesus says there's always a need for people to work for him. Is this work only suitable for Bible experts? Is it only for preachers? Could it be for you?

Matthew 9:35-38

PRAYER: Lord Jesus, as I look at my family and friends, I can see some of them who need you. Please call people to bring them your peace and comfort. And please use me where you need me.

* * * *

JANUARY 20
JULY 20

QUESTION: This is a prophecy of Jesus, appointed to preach good news, written about 700 years before he was born in Bethlehem. Into which group in this reading do you fit?

Isaiah 61:1-3

PRAYER: Thank you, Jesus, that you not only came to Earth specially for people like me – but you came for me.

JANUARY 21
JULY 21

QUESTION: Who is showing you the way in life? Is it your own commonsense, or perhaps your best friend – or the Lord God?

Psalm 25:1-7

PRAYER FROM TODAY'S READING: Show me your ways, O LORD, teach me your paths; Guide me in your truth and teach me, for you are God my Savoir, and my hope is in you all day long.

* * * *

JANUARY 22
JULY 22

QUESTION: Are you ever "hungry" for the wrong things? We all are, at times. What should we be hungry for?

John 6:35-40

PRAYER: My Jesus, I love you, but so often I want the wrong things. Please help me receive the true Bread of Life, and be satisfied.

JANUARY 23
JULY 23

QUESTION: Following Jesus is not always easy, but do you think it's worth the struggle? What have you had to give up to follow him? Is there something else you need to give up to follow him even more closely?

Mark 1:14b-20

PRAYER: Lord, show me if anything is keeping me away from you. Help me give things up that are getting in the way of our relationship.

* * * *

JANUARY 24
JULY 24

QUESTION: Paul is writing to the early church in Rome. How does God demonstrate his great love for us? Clue: The answer is in the last two lines.

Romans 5:1-8

PRAYER SUGGESTION: Thank the Lord for what is written in the last two lines.

JANUARY 25
JULY 25

QUESTION: The prophet Micah, writing 700 years before the birth of Jesus, is looking forward even further – to the time when Jesus will return for ever, destroying evil and bringing peace.

Micah 4:1-5

PRAYER: Jesus, I know you're coming back one day. Help me be ready for your return, and in the meantime stay faithful to you.

* * * *

JANUARY 26
JULY 26

QUESTION: Have you ever felt so troubled that there seems to be no way on? Remember, God is hearing your cries for help. Or are you not crying to him for help – just complaining?

Psalm 18:1-6

PRAYER: Lord God, I love you, but sometimes you feel so far away. Help me understand that you are hearing my cries for help, and please comfort me now.

JANUARY 27
JULY 27

QUESTION: Do you worry about things? Maybe we'd worry less if we were absolutely sure there was a place for us in Heaven. Jesus says we can be sure!

John 14:1-7

PRAYER: Thank you, Lord, that there is a place for me in Heaven. Please help me know that you really are the Way, the Truth and the Life.

* * * *

JANUARY 28
JULY 28

QUESTION: Would you like to hear the voice of God speaking to you out loud? Why did you give that answer?

Matthew 3:13-17

PRAYER: Lord God, help me hear you speaking to me, and please help me listen carefully.

JANUARY 29
JULY 29

QUESTION: Do you know the Sermon on the Mount? Are you sure? Look again at some of the words Jesus spoke, and try to put them into your own words. It's not that easy!

Matthew 5:1-10

PRAYER: Jesus, as I read the words you spoke on the mountainside, please help me understand them more than I do already.

* * * *

JANUARY 30
JULY 30

QUESTION: Who is like God? That's the question the psalmist asks here. But which is more important to him – his troubles, or God's greatness?

Psalm 71:14-21

PRAYER SUGGESTION: Use these opening words of the psalm to praise God: "But as for me, I will always have hope; I will praise you more and more."

JANUARY 31
JULY 31

QUESTION: Do you want to be more pure within? You do? That's a good sign. The time to worry is when we think we're perfect!

Psalm 51:10-17

PRAYER: Lord God, I know I have many things wrong in my life. Please forgive me and help me put things right – with your love and strength.

* * * *

FEBRUARY 1
AUGUST 1

QUESTION: How do you think God helps those who call to him? Note that even "the righteous man has many troubles." The answer to this puzzle seems to be that "the Lord redeems his servants" – he doesn't condemn them. In other words, some answers to prayer seem to be rooted in eternity rather than giving a short-term fix.

Psalm 34:15-22

PRAYER: Lord God, my Heavenly Father, you know my needs. Whatever answer I get, help me have faith that even if things don't make sense now, I will understand it all in Heaven.

FEBRUARY 2
AUGUST 2

QUESTION: The Israelites are facing a dangerous enemy. The Lord is telling the people that the enemy will be defeated before the attack even begins. How can we see here that the people trusted God?

2 Chronicles 20:17-21

PRAYER: Lord God, when things ahead look threatening, help me trust you and give praise to your name, even before the enemy is defeated.

* * * *

FEBRUARY 3
AUGUST 3

QUESTION: It's great to see Christians getting on well together. But is that all we need do? What about getting on with people who don't like us?

Matthew 5:43-48

PRAYER: Thank you, Lord, for Christian friends. Help me get on well with them. But especially I need you to help me get on with people with whom I don't see eye to eye.

FEBRUARY 4
AUGUST 4

QUESTION: Why would a loving father give something dangerous to his child? So why do you sometimes wonder if your loving Heavenly Father is caring for you?

Luke 11:9-13

PRAYER: Loving Heavenly Father, please give me all I really need, especially give me the Holy Spirit. Help me trust you at all times.

* * * *

FEBRUARY 5
AUGUST 5

QUESTION: Do you expect to find God in all sorts of situations in your life? Or is your life divided into two compartments: Sunday, and the rest of the week when you're alone?

Exodus 3:1-6

PRAYER: When you speak to me in unexpected places, Lord, please help me hear your voice. And help me hear it clearly.

FEBRUARY 6
AUGUST 6

QUESTION: Christmas is long gone, Easter is a few weeks off, so this is a good time to remember why the Saviour came. In this reading Jesus is about to be arrested and taken for trial and crucifixion. Would you have stayed awake with him? Are there things you mean to do for God, but never get them done? Jesus understands and forgives, but do you think it makes him sad?

Mark 14:32-38

PRAYER: Jesus, please help me be more wide awake when it comes to doing things for you, and please forgive me for the times I've failed you.

* * * *

FEBRUARY 7
AUGUST 7

QUESTION: As you read this, decide what you think are the most important words spoken. Are they what Peter says, what God says or what Jesus says? I think we can rule out Peter!

Matthew 17:1b-8

PRAYER: God, my Heavenly Father, help me listen to what Jesus says. And help me not to be afraid.

FEBRUARY 8
AUGUST 8

QUESTION: Why do you think Jesus asked the blind men what they wanted him to do? Surely it was obvious! Maybe they needed to tell him their problem so they could think about what they needed most.

Matthew 20:29-34

PRAYER SUGGESTION: If you've been praying to Jesus for help for a long time, try asking again. But this time tell Jesus more about your problem.

* * * *

FEBRUARY 9
AUGUST 9

QUESTION: "What must I do to be saved?" How would you answer that question if someone asked you?

Acts 16:25-34

PRAYER: Help me, Lord, to be as ready as Paul and Silas when the jailer asked them how he could be saved.

FEBRUARY 10
AUGUST 10

QUESTION: Does this reading mean that we mustn't ask Jesus questions? Or does it mean that whatever we ask, he'll have the right answer?

Mark 12:28-34

PRAYER SUGGESTION: If you have something on your mind, talk it over with Jesus now. But be ready to hear his voice – however he chooses to answer you.

* * * *

FEBRUARY 11
AUGUST 11

QUESTION: We face setbacks all though life, and maybe some setbacks are extremely serious. Do you think Moses' mother had any idea of the great blessing that would come from the cruel order from the pharaoh, that all male Jewish babies like hers must be killed?

Exodus 2:1-6a
Continued tomorrow

PRAYER: Lord God, I'm never going to understand your great ways. Help me trust you when the way ahead seems dark and hopeless.

FEBRUARY 12
AUGUST 12

Continued from yesterday

QUESTION: Could Moses' mother have put her son into a lowly position in the pharaoh's palace by herself? Could she have got him adopted as the pharaoh's son? God could – and did!

Exodus 2:6b-10

PRAYER SUGGESTION: Tell God how great he is, and ask him to increase your trust in him.

* * * *

FEBRUARY 13
AUGUST 13

QUESTION: Why did the Christian faith get off to such a quick start, in so many countries? How many people heard and listened in this reading? And that's just the men!

Acts 4:1-7
Continued tomorrow

PRAYER: Thank you, Lord, for men like Peter and John who were used by you with such power. Please continue to use men and women, of all ages, to carry on your work today.

FEBRUARY 14
AUGUST 14

Continued from yesterday
QUESTION: Peter was a powerful preacher. Where did he get his power from?

Acts 4:8-12
PRAYER SUGGESTION: Think prayerfully about these words: "Salvation is found in no one else, for there is no other name under Heaven given to men by which we must be saved." And now give thanks.

* * * *

FEBRUARY 15
AUGUST 15

QUESTION: Many Christians still feel that they've not been completely forgiven. Are you one of them? There really is no need to feel like this – if you believe these promises.

Psalm 103:8-13

PRAYER: Heavenly Father, please be a true and loving father to me. Have compassion on me and give me a definite assurance of full forgiveness.

FEBRUARY 16
AUGUST 16

QUESTION: John knew Jesus – he worked and travelled with him. John writes here, "There can be no greater comfort than assurance of forgiveness and eternal life." Do you really understand the astonishing meaning of the word "assurance"?

John 1:10-14

PRAYER: Lord Jesus, help me recognize you more and more each day, and I thank you now for the wonderful promise of forgiveness and eternal life.

* * * *

FEBRUARY 17
AUGUST 17

QUESTION: This is a simple psalm, but can you notice the picture language used? Can you picture God riding the "ancient skies"? Can you hear him in the thunder? Of course, God is God and nature is nature, but it is all God's creation – so praise him whenever you see nature's wonders.

Psalm 68:32-35

PRAYER: Heavenly Father, thank you for your wonderful creation. Help me understand more about you through the amazing things that happen all around.

FEBRUARY 18
AUGUST 18

QUESTION: This sounds a bit of a roller coaster ride for Jesus. The Holy Spirit comes – and then Satan tempts him. Do you sometimes find that peaks in your faith are followed by problems? Could God be using difficulties to strengthen your faith?

Mark 1:9-13

PRAYER: Heavenly Father, my faith seems to go in ups and downs. Many times the downs are my own fault, but when I can see no reason, please use the time to strengthen my faith.

* * * *

FEBRUARY 19
AUGUST 19

QUESTION: Do you know why Jesus is called the Lamb of God? Big clue – in the Old Testament lambs were used in sacrifice.

John 1:35-42

PRAYER: Jesus, please help me recognize you as the perfect Lamb of God, sacrificed for me so that all my guilt and sin has been taken away, and now help me follow you more closely.

FEBRUARY 20
AUGUST 20

QUESTION: Jesus has risen from the grave after his death on the cross, and returned to Heaven. The Holy Spirit has come to the disciples and filled them with boldness and power. So what does Peter do?

Acts 3:6-10
Continued tomorrow

PRAYER: Holy Spirit, please come and fill me with boldness and power, so I can reach out to people in need.

* * * *

FEBRUARY 21
AUGUST 21

Continued from yesterday
QUESTION: God doesn't just use Peter to heal a man who is in great physical need, he uses Peter to do something else – something even more important. What?

Acts 3:11-16

PRAYER: Holy Spirit, I need the boldness and power you gave Peter, so I can talk about you with other people.

FEBRUARY 22
AUGUST 22

QUESTION: Jesus is not talking to his disciples about his real body and blood, but about receiving him as Saviour. Why do you think some people might not like to hear these words? Why do you think Christians get great comfort from them?

John 6:53-59

PRAYER: Jesus, please may I understand what it means to feed on the true "Bread", and know that you are living in me. Make these words a great comfort to me.

* * * *

FEBRUARY 23
AUGUST 23

QUESTION: Sometimes Christians get a little too self-confident, and forget that we need God all day and all night – until things go wrong. And it's only then that we turn to prayer! Is this you?

Psalm 30:4-12

PRAYER: Heavenly Father, forgive me for relying on my own strength. May my heart sing to you and not be silent.

FEBRUARY 24
AUGUST 24

QUESTION: Jesus has been denouncing the towns and cities that have not accepted him. Now he offers an invitation to the ordinary people. Can you put a yoke onto your shoulders without first putting down the things you're holding? Think about it.

Matthew 11:25b-30

PRAYER: Lord Jesus, as I take your yoke upon my shoulders, please take my own burdens from me. Then give my soul the rest that you've promised.

* * * *

FEBRUARY 25
AUGUST 25

QUESTION: Think about the things that sometimes make you afraid. What do you fear most? Is the remedy here?

Psalm 27:1-6
Continued tomorrow

PRAYER SUGGESTION: Ask God to help make these words yours: "In the day of trouble he will keep me safe in his dwelling; he will hide me in the shelter of his tabernacle and set me high upon a rock."

FEBRUARY 26
AUGUST 26

Continued from yesterday
QUESTION: Some people wait for God to show himself to them – without bothering to look for him. Is this a mistake you sometimes make?

Psalm 27:7-14

PRAYER: Lord God, when you sometimes seem so far away, please help me to keep calling to you, and I ask you to hear my prayers today.

* * * *

FEBRUARY 27
AUGUST 27

QUESTION: How many good things are free in life? Salvation is, but many people are too proud to accept it as a gift – they think they have to work for it. How sad!

Revelation 22:12-17

PRAYER: Thank you, Jesus, that you have given me clean robes, and covered me in your righteousness.

FEBRUARY 28
AUGUST 28

QUESTION: Do you have a few dark corners in your life? Everyone does, but Jesus wants to shine his light in them – to bring you comfort and relief. Just ask him to fill you with his wonderful light.

Luke 11:33-36

PRAYER: Jesus, my Saviour, you know the things that are still wrong in my life. Please fill me with your holy light, so that there will be no more dark corners.

* * * *

FEBRUARY 29
AUGUST 29

QUESTION: Which is the hardest of these things to do: Love sincerely, hate evil, cling to what is good – or be devoted to one another in brotherly love? Did you say the last one?

Romans 12:9-18

PRAYER: Lord, you know that I find it hard to achieve brotherly love by myself. Please help me live at peace with everyone, especially other Christians.

AUGUST 30

QUESTION: Maybe everyone knows that there are two gates we can go through in life – a narrow one and a wide one. Are you walking with Jesus on the Narrow Way, or walking by yourself on the Broad Way?

Matthew 7:7-13

PRAYER SUGGESTION: Think for a moment about which gate you've entered. It's not too late to change. Either thank Jesus that you've entered through the narrow gate, or ask him to lead you to it.

* * * *

AUGUST 31

QUESTION: Do you sometimes find it hard to hear the Lord's voice? Maybe you're not listening in the right place!

Psalm 29:3-11

PRAYER: Lord, help me hear your voice in many different places, for you are the mighty God of Heaven.

MARCH 1
SEPTEMBER 1

QUESTION: After the crucifixion, Thomas wouldn't believe that Jesus was alive – unless he could touch him. Do you think it would help if you could see Jesus face to face, and touch him?

John 20:24-30

PRAYER: I know I cannot see you yet, Jesus, so please help me believe in you at all times, and please increase my faith.

* * * *

MARCH 2
SEPTEMBER 2

QUESTION: The lepers called out, "Jesus, Master, have pity on us!" And Jesus took pity on them. How grateful were they? How grateful are you for what Jesus has done in your life?

Luke 17:11-19

PRAYER SUGGESTION: Maybe there was a time when you told Jesus how grateful you are for what he has done for you. Take this opportunity to thank him again today – and again tomorrow.

MARCH 3
SEPTEMBER 3

QUESTION: The people are hungry, but it looks as though Jesus is not going to help them. Have you ever felt God is "testing" you?

John 6:1-9
Continued tomorrow

PRAYER: Forgive me, Lord, for not always trusting you. Please help my trust in you to grow stronger, and not weaker, through times of trouble.

* * * *

MARCH 4
SEPTEMBER 4
Continued from yesterday
QUESTION: The people think Jesus is "the Prophet", and they want to make him king by force. But surely Jesus is already the King, but how different is he from the king these people expected?

John 6:10-15
Continued tomorrow

PRAYER: Lord Jesus, help me understand what sort of King you are. And please be King of my life.

MARCH 5
SEPTEMBER 5
Continued from yesterday

QUESTION: The disciples are not only scared of the storm, they are scared of Jesus when they see him. Can you hear his voice today telling you not to be afraid? Spend a little time listening after you read these verses.

John 6:16-21
Continued tomorrow

PRAYER: Jesus, help me not to be afraid, but to trust you all the time – even when I think I have a very good reason to be frightened. Please come into every part of my life.

* * * *

MARCH 6
SEPTEMBER 6
Continued from yesterday
QUESTION: Are you following Jesus for what you can get, or simply because you believe and trust in him?

John 6:25-29

PRAYER: Jesus, please help me not to wonder what I can get out of life, but just to believe and trust in you.

MARCH 7
SEPTEMBER 7

QUESTION: Did it take you a long time before you followed Jesus, or did you start to follow him as soon as he called you? Or is he still waiting for you to start?

Matthew 4:18-23

PRAYER SUGGESTION: Look at the question at the top of this page, and pray about your answer.

* * * *

MARCH 8
SEPTEMBER 8

QUESTION: Does it make you uncomfortable to learn that God knows all about you? Or does the thought fill you with wonder that he cares so much for you?

Psalm 139:1-6
Continued tomorrow

PRAYER: Help me, Lord, to feel comfortable knowing that you are always close to me. Help me see that you are a loving father.

MARCH 9
SEPTEMBER 9
Continued from yesterday

QUESTION: Look at yesterday's question. Do you have a different answer now? Will you have a different answer after today's reading?

Psalm 139:7-12

PRAYER SUGGESTION: Tell God your real feelings about these verses. Then thank him that he will never leave you alone.

* * * *

MARCH 10
SEPTEMBER 10

QUESTION: Paul tells the early Christians in Philippi not to be anxious about anything. Is it that easy?

Philippians 4:4-9

PRAYER: God of peace, please be with me. Help me trust you for everything in life, even when things are difficult.

EASTER

THERE ARE SPECIAL EASTER READINGS ON PAGE 101, STARTING ON PALM SUNDAY, THE SUNDAY BEFORE EASTER

YOU MAY LIKE TO USE THEM WHENEVER EASTER COMES THIS YEAR

MARCH 11
SEPTEMBER 11

QUESTION: Does it surprise you that someone can say their sins are forgiven and covered? Can you say this? And mean it?

Psalm 32:1-7

PRAYER: Lord God, may I know for sure that you have forgiven my sins. Please forgive me now, not because I deserve forgiveness, but because you took the punishment for me.

* * * *

MARCH 12
SEPTEMBER 12

QUESTION: Jesus has just fed 5,000 people. Do you think the disciples were more afraid of the storm, or of seeing Jesus? Why don't we always recognize Jesus when he comes to help us?

Matthew 14:22-27
Continued tomorrow

PRAYER: Lord Jesus, please help me recognize you when you come to help me, and not turn away from you.

MARCH 13
SEPTEMBER 13
Continued from yesterday

QUESTION: Do you think Jesus is angry with Peter for not having much faith? Do you think Jesus understands why we often doubt?

Matthew 14:28-36

PRAYER: Jesus, please understand that my faith is often weak, and I sometimes doubt that you are in charge of my life. Help me trust you more and more each day.

* * * *

MARCH 14
SEPTEMBER 14

QUESTION: Why do you think people sometimes get angry with Jesus? Is it because they don't ask him directly who he is, or because they don't like his answer?

John 7:37-44

PRAYER: Lord, there are times when I feel so dry inside, and far away from you. Please tell me more about who you are, and fill me with your streams of living water.

MARCH 15
SEPTEMBER 15

QUESTION: We all tend to worry about things. Does it sound as though we're wasting our time worrying?

Matthew 6:25-29
Continued tomorrow

PRAYER: Lord, I do worry from time to time. Sometimes I worry a lot. Please help me trust in you, whatever happens.

* * * *

MARCH 16
SEPTEMBER 16
Continued from yesterday
QUESTION: Look back at yesterday's question. Do you feel happier about things now?

Matthew 6:31-34

PRAYER: Heavenly Father, please help me put you first in everything I do in life, and to put you first in everything that happens to me.

MARCH 17
SEPTEMBER 17

QUESTION: Sometimes people grow up in such a Christian environment that the teaching they hear doesn't have any special meaning. Was this a problem for the people here? Or did they think Jesus was too ordinary to be the Son of God?

Matthew 13:53-58

PRAYER: Jesus, help me see exactly who you are: the Son of God, the Saviour of the world – and my own Saviour.

* * * *

MARCH 18
SEPTEMBER 18

QUESTION: This is one of David's psalms. Who does David say made the Heavens? Are you really looking forward to the time when the whole world will give God glory? Looking forward to it all the time?

1 Chronicles 16:23-29
Continued tomorrow

PRAYER: Lord God, you are great, and most worthy of praise. May the time come when all the nations praise your holy name.

MARCH 19
SEPTEMBER 19
Continued from yesterday

QUESTION: One day all this will be true. When? Clue: fourth paragraph.

1 Chronicles 16:30-36

PRAYER SUGGESTION: Use the last three lines as praise to the Lord.

* * * *

MARCH 20
SEPTEMBER 20

QUESTION: How long does God's covenant of love last? A few years, a thousand years – or for ever?

Deuteronomy 7:6-9

PRAYER: Thank you, Heavenly Father, that you are a faithful God, and thank you that you keep your promise of love.

MARCH 21
SEPTEMBER 21

QUESTION: Do you sometimes need to have something explained several times before you catch on? If so, you must be like the disciples!

John 12:12-16

PRAYER: Help me, Jesus, to not only listen to what you tell me, but to understand it as well.

* * * *

MARCH 22
SEPTEMBER 22

QUESTION: What are the most important truths of the Christian faith that Paul highlights here?

1 Corinthians 15:1-7

PRAYER: Heavenly Father, thank you that "Christ died for my sins according to the Scriptures, that he was buried, that he was raised on the third day according to the Scriptures."

MARCH 23
SEPTEMBER 23

QUESTION: David says that without God he can do nothing – not even see the way ahead. Is this true for you?

2 Samuel 22:29-33

PRAYER: Thank you, Heavenly Father, that you turn my darkness into light. I ask you to show me the way that I should be taking now.

* * * *

MARCH 24
SEPTEMBER 24

QUESTION: No one knows what Heaven will be like, but do you have a picture of it in your mind? Is it like this?

Revelation 21:21-27

PRAYER SUGGESTION: Is your name written in the Lamb's book of life? If so, now is the time to say thank you again. If you're in doubt, make sure of it – by asking Jesus into your life.

MARCH 25
SEPTEMBER 25

QUESTION: We can look in the Old Testament and read about some of God's mighty works. Do you still think of God in the same terms today? Isn't God the same yesterday, today and for ever?

Psalm 68:4-10

PRAYER SUGGESTION: Ask God for an abundant shower to refresh you. And then praise him for his greatness.

* * * *

MARCH 26
SEPTEMBER 26

QUESTION: Do you take time to listen to God – in a time of silence?

1 Kings 19:9-13

LORD was not in the wind. After the wind there was an earthquake, but the LORD was not in the earthquake.

PRAYER: Help me take time to listen to you, Lord, and let me hear your gentle whisper above all the noise and bustle of life.

MARCH 27
SEPTEMBER 27

QUESTION: We often take this story of the lost sheep for granted, because we know it so well. Did Jesus come looking for you when you were lost?

Matthew 18:10-14

PRAYER: Thank you, Jesus, that even though I once was lost, you came looking for me and carried me safely home in your arms.

* * * *

MARCH 28
SEPTEMBER 28

QUESTION: Who is worthy enough to reach down and untie Jesus' sandals? What does "worthy" mean? Probably "deserving" would fit best here.

Mark 1:4-8

PRAYER: Lord, I don't deserve anything from you. I'm not worthy to do anything for you, but I know you've accepted me just as I am. So I want to say thank you.

MARCH 29
SEPTEMBER 29

QUESTION: If your life is in God's hands, why do you sometimes feel impatient?

Psalm 37:1-7a

PRAYER: Please, Lord, help me wait patiently for you. Help me trust in you, whatever is happening in my life.

* * * *

MARCH 30
SEPTEMBER 30

QUESTION: If you get an invitation to a party, and you want to go, what do you need to do before going? Hint: Something about accepting the invitation!

Revelation 19:4-9

PRAYER: Thank you, Jesus, for the amazing invitation to the wedding feast in Heaven. Yes please, I'll be there!

MARCH 31

QUESTION: Jonah is in deep trouble, literally, but where does his salvation come from?

Jonah 2:5-9

PRAYER: Lord, sometimes I cling to worthless things, trying to get help from them in my life. Please forgive me, and let me always turn to you in times of trouble.

EASTER REMINDER

THERE ARE SPECIAL EASTER READINGS, ON PAGE 101 STARTING FOR PALM SUNDAY, THE SUNDAY BEFORE EASTER

YOU MAY LIKE TO USE THEM WHENEVER EASTER COMES THIS YEAR

APRIL 1
OCTOBER 1

QUESTION: This is Peter, the disciple who let Jesus down before the crucifixion. Look what's happened to him since then – major apostle and Spirit-filled preacher. What does he put this change down to? Clue: See third paragraph of this reading.

2 Peter 1:1-8

PRAYER: Lord Jesus, may I have the qualities mentioned here in increasing measure, so that I may be useful to you.

* * * *

APRIL 2
OCTOBER 2

QUESTION: Are there times when you don't understand God? Of course we should pray for wisdom and insight, though we can hardly expect to know God's mind – but are there times when all you can do is trust him?

Isaiah 55:9-13

PRAYER: Thank you, Lord God, that when your word goes out into the earth, it is heard and people respond to it. May your word fill me with understanding.

APRIL 3
OCTOBER 3

QUESTION: Are sometimes afraid that Jesus may let go of you? Read here how no one can snatch you out of his hand.

John 10:22-30

PRAYER: Jesus, I have heard so many times who you are. Help me understand that I am one of your sheep, and that you have given me eternal life.

* * * *

APRIL 4
OCTOBER 4

QUESTION: The prophet Isaiah sometimes looks forward to the birth of Jesus, and at other times to when Jesus will return and take us all to Heaven. Which is this?

Isaiah 2:1-5

PRAYER: Lord Jesus, help me look forward to your return. And if it happens my lifetime, please let me be ready to greet you when you come.

APRIL 5
OCTOBER 5

QUESTION: Does sin matter? Here is a well-known story, but make sure you read the ending carefully.

John 8:2-11

PRAYER: Lord Jesus, so often I do wrong things. Please forgive me, and help me keep so close to you so that I may know your love all the time.

* * * *

APRIL 6
OCTOBER 6

QUESTION: Do you find it helps to worship God by singing his praises?

Psalm 63:1-8

PRAYER SUGGESTION: Can you say with the Psalmist, "I will praise you as long as I live, and in your name I will lift up my hands"? It may feel strange at first, but try lifting up your hands to the Lord now – even if you don't sing!

APRIL 7
OCTOBER 7

QUESTION: Imagine Jesus is standing in front of you, and you need his healing touch. Would you dare reach out and touch him? Have you ever reached out?

Mark 5:25-34

PRAYER SUGGESTION: If you have a special need, reach out and touch Jesus now – and tell him exactly what you want. Now think about what you've just asked for, and make sure it's the right thing. If it's not, rephrase the prayer.

* * * *

APRIL 8
OCTOBER 8

QUESTION: Do you know that Jesus is the Lamb of God, sacrificed for you on the cross?

Revelation 7:9-12
Continued tomorrow

PRAYER SUGGESTION: Thank the Lord God that your salvation comes from him, and that Jesus is the Lamb, sacrificed for your forgiveness.

APRIL 9
OCTOBER 9

Continued from yesterday
QUESTION: Do you feel excited to know that there will be so many people in Heaven with you that you won't be able to count them all? Who will be there that you know?

Revelation 7:13-17

PRAYER: Lord Jesus, please help me be welcoming now to Christians from all over the world, and not just think of myself. And thank you that every tear will be wiped away in Heaven.

* * * *

APRIL 10
OCTOBER 10

QUESTION: Do you sometimes think God isn't bothered about you, or do you find it easy to trust in his unfailing love? Think for a moment what "unfailing" means.

Psalm 13:1-6

PRAYER: Please help me, Creator God, to trust in your unfailing love. And help me rejoice in the salvation he has given you.

APRIL 11
OCTOBER 11

QUESTION: John has a wonderful vision of Heaven and the return of Jesus some time in the future. John sounds excited by what he sees. Do his words excite you?

Revelation 1:4-8

PRAYER: Lord, you love me and have freed me from my sins. Please help me be excited about it, and want to share it with others.

* * * *

APRIL 12
OCTOBER 12

QUESTION: A thief enters a house through a window – the owner enters through the front door with a key. Jesus says he is the "Gate". What happens to people who enter through that Gate?

John 10:1-10
Continued tomorrow

PRAYER: Jesus, I know you are the Gate. Thank you for giving me life. Please give me life to the full.

APRIL 13
OCTOBER 13

Continued from yesterday
QUESTION: Jesus says that the good shepherd lays down his life for his sheep – that he gives his life. If you are one of his sheep, have you thanked him for giving his life for you?

John 10:11-18
PRAYER: Jesus, you are indeed the Good Shepherd. Thank you for giving your life for me – on the cross. And thank you for making me your very own child.

* * * *

APRIL 14
OCTOBER 14

QUESTION: Do you sometimes wonder if the stories of Jesus are reliable? Peter was there with Jesus, and wants us to be sure that nothing was invented.

2 Peter 1:16-21

PRAYER: Thank you, Jesus, for the story of your life in the Bible. Thank you for the early Christians who risked their lives to tell it to others, and thank you for people like Peter who gave their lives to tell it.

APRIL 15
OCTOBER 15

QUESTION: John is telling us that he saw and touched Jesus while he was here on Earth. But what is John telling us (proclaiming) about Jesus?

1 John 1:1-4
Continued tomorrow

PRAYER: Lord God, we have not seen you yet, but we ask that we will have fellowship with you today: Father, Son and Holy Spirit.

* * * *

APRIL 16
OCTOBER 16

Continued from yesterday
1 JOHN 1:5-9

QUESTION: If someone claimed they had never sinned, would you believe them? If someone said they knew their sins were forgiven, could you believe them?

PRAYER: Thank you, Jesus, for this wonderful promise, that if I confess my sins – and I sin so often – that you really will forgive me.

APRIL 17
OCTOBER 17

QUESTION: Instead of always asking for things, do you sometimes just spend time with God praising him for who he is?

Psalm 33:1-9

PRAYER SUGGESTION: Instead of asking, spend a short time praising God. If you're unsure what to say, use some words from this Psalm.

* * * *

APRIL 18
OCTOBER 18

QUESTION: No one can come to Jesus without first realizing that they need him. Have you opened the door and asked him into your life?

Revelation 3:17-21

PRAYER SUGGESTION: If you haven't done it yet, now is the time to ask Jesus into your life. If you've already done it, thank him once again that he came in.

APRIL 19
OCTOBER 19

QUESTION: The Bible tells us that God's love is unfailing. Could you put a price on unfailing love? The Psalmist couldn't.

Psalm 36:5-10

PRAYER: Lord, please may I drink from the fountain of life, and see your light on the way ahead.

* * * *

APRIL 20
OCTOBER 20

QUESTION: Are you guaranteed a place with Jesus in Heaven? You are – if you've responded to the gospel of salvation!

Ephesians 2:13-17

PRAYER SUGGESTION: Ask that the God of our Lord Jesus Christ, the glorious Father, may give you the Spirit of wisdom and revelation, so that you may know him better..

APRIL 21
OCTOBER 21

QUESTION: Where can you find out more about Jesus? How about the teaching in the Bible!

2 Thessalonians 2:13-17

PRAYER SUGGESTION: Ask Jesus to help you stand firm in the faith, and give you encouragement to go on trusting him.

* * * *

APRIL 22
OCTOBER 22

QUESTION: How often do you report back to Jesus about what you've done?

Mark 6:30-34

PRAYER: Jesus, help me remember to talk with you about the things I've done. And when I'm wandering like a lost sheep, please teach me new things so that I may return home refreshed.

APRIL 23
OCTOBER 23

QUESTION: As the psalmist says here, you can be filled with joy at the thought of being with the Lord. Who or what do you think about at night? Maybe that is your god!

Psalm 16:5-11

PRAYER: Help me, Lord, to rejoice at the thought of being secure with you, and let me be filled with joy both in the day and at night.

* * * *

APRIL 24
OCTOBER 24

QUESTION: Micah says that someone special would be coming from Bethlehem – but we now know that the people had to wait 700 years after he wrote these words. Was it worth the wait?

Micah 5:2-5a

PRAYER: Lord, be my shepherd and lead me in the right path, and please be my peace.

APRIL 25
OCTOBER 25

QUESTION: Do you sometimes wonder what people would think about you, if they could see what you are really like on the inside? We all have hidden faults – but God can forgive and heal if we ask.

Psalm 19:7-14

PRAYER SUGGESTION: Ask God to forgive your hidden faults, and ask him to give you his peace.

* * * *

APRIL 26
OCTOBER 26

QUESTION: "Thank you, Jesus, that I'm not like all these people who don't know you." Is this a good thing to pray – or not?"

Luke 18:9-14

PRAYER: Thank you, Jesus, that even though I deserved nothing from you, you heard me when I called to you, and took me just as I was. Please hold me tightly in your hand for ever.

APRIL 27
OCTOBER 27

QUESTION: Jesus died on the cross, but he came alive again. He's alive now. Could you share this news with someone if they asked you what you believe?

1 Peter 3:13-18

PRAYER: Thank you, Jesus, that you died on the cross to take my sins. Help me to understand it so well that I can explain this to anyone who asks what I believe.

* * * *

APRIL 28
OCTOBER 28

QUESTION: When can you feel confident enough to approach Jesus? When you think you've done well – or when you realize just how weak you are?

Hebrews 4:13-16

PRAYER SUGGESTION: Thank the Lord Jesus that he is able to sympathize with your weakness, then "approach the throne with confidence so that you may receive mercy and find grace to help you in your time of need."

APRIL 29
OCTOBER 29

QUESTION: When Jesus found a man with special needs, why do you think he wanted the man to tell him what he wanted him to do?

Luke 18:35-43

PRAYER SUGGESTION: Rather than vague prayers, like "Lord, please bless me," we should ask for specific things. Tell Jesus now exactly what you want him to do, and why you want him to do it.

* * * *

APRIL 30
OCTOBER 30

QUESTION: When things get difficult in life, who or what do you trust in – strong things like "horses and chariots", or the Lord God?

Psalm 20:1-9

PRAYER: Help me, Lord, to trust in your mighty name, and may I shout for joy when I know your strength.

OCTOBER 31

QUESTION: Did David praise God on his own, or with others? Praising God with other Christians is a great way to honour his name.

1 Chronicles 29:10-13

PRAYER: Lord God, I give you thanks that you are wonderful, reliable and in charge of all things. Help me praise your holy name.

MAY 1
NOVEMBER 1

QUESTION: Is God loving? Yes. Is God awesome? Yes. Can we really understand God? No, not really – should we be trying to understand him better?

Psalm 89:1-8

PRAYER SUGGESTION: Ask God to help you understand more about him, and to love him more and more.

* * * *

MAY 2
NOVEMBER 2

QUESTION: When we give money to those in need, we often work out how much we can afford. It's the same with our time. We keep back plenty for ourselves. How much should we give to Jesus?

Mark 12:41-44

PRAYER: Lord Jesus, you gave your life for me on the cross, yet I often hold back from giving to you. Please take more of what I have, including my time and money – and also have more of my love.

MAY 3
NOVEMBER 3

QUESTION: We all like getting presents. If you're really thirsty, what's the most obvious thing you would want? Is it a luxury present, or a necessity?

Revelation 21:1-7

PRAYER: Jesus, I want to thank you that not only will all the pain and trouble of this life be done away with in Heaven, but that you will give me the water of life as a gift.

* * * *

MAY 4
NOVEMBER 4

QUESTION: What things in life make you feel afraid? What things make you glad?

Psalm 46:1-7

PRAYER: Lord God, I know that you are with me, that you are like a fortress for me. Please help me understand this better.

MAY 5
NOVEMBER 5

QUESTION: Do you consider other people better than yourself? No? Surely it's sometimes hard not to! So is the answer, yes, sometimes? Maybe you'll be encouraged to know that Jesus managed to do it.

Philippians 2:1-11

PRAYER: Lord, you know how hard it is to put other people first, but please help me learn from you, when you came to die for me on the cross.

* * * *

MAY 6
NOVEMBER 6

QUESTION: This is a wonderful story, but is it possible for people today to believe, without seeing "miraculous signs and wonders"? Millions do!

John 4:46-53

PRAYER: Lord God, it would be so much easier to believe if we could see signs like this. Help me have a stronger faith, and to trust you.

MAY 7
NOVEMBER 7

QUESTION: Is it possible to be "saved" just a little bit? Or is it all or nothing?

Hebrews 7:23-27

PRAYER: Thank you, Jesus, that you took my sins on the cross, and took them completely, and made me all yours.

* * * *

MAY 8
NOVEMBER 8

QUESTION: Maybe you know the words of this Psalm very well, but have you thought about what they really mean for you?

Psalm 23:1-6

PRAYER: Lord God, I know you love me, but I want to be secure in your promise that I will live in your house for ever.

MAY 9
NOVEMBER 9

QUESTION: Luke, the writer of Acts, has now joined the Apostles and is writing about what he saw and heard. Was the Christian gospel just for men?

Acts 16:13-15

PRAYER: Thank you, Jesus, for open hearts. Please open the hearts of those of my family and friends who have yet to receive you as Lord and Saviour.

* * * *

MAY 10
NOVEMBER 10

QUESTION: Who is Jesus, that he can forgive sins? Can you be sure that he has forgiven yours?

Luke 5:17-20

PRAYER: Jesus, I know that when you say something you mean it. Help me take it in when you say my sins are forgiven.

MAY 11
NOVEMBER 11

QUESTION: How does Paul say you will be saved? Can it really be as easy as that? It is, which is why some people think it's too easy, and keep trying to earn their salvation.

Romans 10:8-13

PRAYER SUGGESTION: If you've already confessed with your mouth that "Jesus is Lord," and believe in your heart that God raised him from the dead, then thank him for your salvation. If you've not thanked him, now may be the time to do it – and stop trying to be "good enough."

* * * *

MAY 12
NOVEMBER 12

QUESTION: Have you ever prayed for the whole world? The Psalmist has!

Psalm 67:1-7

PRAYER SUGGESTION: Try using some words from this Psalm as a prayer for the whole world.

MAY 13
NOVEMBER 13

QUESTION: Do you know who the King of Glory is? If you do, why is there any need to be anxious in life?

Psalm 24:1-10

PRAYER: Please give me forgiveness, Lord, and wash me clean so that I may lift up my hands in praise before you.

* * * *

MAY 14
NOVEMBER 14

QUESTION: Jesus is talking to his disciples, telling them that he has to go away. Why does Jesus tell them they'll be better off when he's gone, than they would be if he stays with them where they can see him? Clue: The Holy Spirit can be with each one of us wherever we are, rather than having to meet him in one place.

John 14:15-21

PRAYER: Holy Spirit, come to me now and give me the certainty of the presence of Jesus.

MAY 15
NOVEMBER 15

QUESTION: Do you think that God is only with you sometimes – or is he always holding you by the hand?

Psalm 73:23-28

PRAYER: Lord God, whom have I in Heaven but you? Please hold me tightly by the hand.

* * * *

MAY 16
NOVEMBER 16

QUESTION: Paul has heard of the faith of the early Christians in Colossae. Has anyone heard of your faith? Maybe you should tell someone soon.

Colossians 1:3-8
Continued tomorrow

PRAYER: Dear Lord, please help me share my faith with my family and friends. Sometimes it seems so hard, but with your strength I can do it.

MAY 17
NOVEMBER 17

Continued from yesterday
QUESTION: When you think of what Jesus has done for you on the cross, bringing you into his kingdom, do you think you can still stay silent?

Colossians 1:9-14

PRAYER: Help me, Lord, to share my faith, and help me keep praying for my family and friends, that they will find you as their Lord and Saviour.

* * * *

MAY 18
NOVEMBER 18

QUESTION: Can you say the first two lines of this Psalm and mean them? Try saying them aloud now.

Psalm 8:1-9
PRAYER: Heavenly Father, your creation is wonderful, and when I look at the things you have made it makes me feel so small. So I want to thank you for your great love for me.

MAY 19
NOVEMBER 19

QUESTION: How good do you need to be to be saved? How bad do you need to be to be saved? Or is it irrelevant which you are?

Titus 3:4-8

PRAYER SUGGESTION: Read through the passage again, and consider before God how you can devote yourself to doing what is good. And thank God that he took you as you were, and didn't consider your so-called "righteousness" – because you'd be in real trouble if he had!

* * * *

MAY 20
NOVEMBER 20

QUESTION: It can be easy to say that God is powerful, but what is he more powerful than? How mighty do you think he is? How mighty is all mighty?

Psalm 93:1-5

PRAYER: Dear God, my Heavenly Father, as I come before you in awe, please help me feel your great love for me.

MAY 21
NOVEMBER 21

QUESTION: Do you sometimes feel that all life is a struggle against things that are bad? If so, listen carefully to Paul's advice here.

Ephesians 6:10-17

PRAYER: Lord, please help me understand more about your armour, and to put it on at all times. Help me remember that I am not on my own in life.

* * * *

MAY 22
NOVEMBER 22

QUESTION: Paul didn't think of himself as much of a preacher, but whenever he preached people turned to Jesus. So where did his power come from?

1 Corinthians 2:1-5

PRAYER: Lord, when I share the good news with others, may they not hear my voice, but yours.

MAY 23
NOVEMBER 23

QUESTION: Do you sometimes feel too proud or too stubborn to accept any help from God?

John 13:4-9

PRAYER: Lord, forgive me for not always wanting your help. Please help me in everything I do, and help me through all my life. Wash me clean, I pray.

* * * *

MAY 24
NOVEMBER 24

QUESTION: Abraham seems to have settled down to a comfortable old age. If so, he had no idea what major changes the future was about to bring. Did he say he was too old and tired to do anything when God called him?

Genesis 12:1-5

PRAYER: Heavenly Father, help me hear your voice. Help me, too, to be willing to make changes in my life.

MAY 25
NOVEMBER 25

QUESTION: The Psalmist here has been going through a time of great trouble. What did he do about it?

Psalm 116:1-7

PRAYER: Heavenly Father, please help me be quick to pray to you when I need you, because I often forget to call out. And please help me talk to you at all times, both when life is easy and when it is hard.

* * * *

MAY 26
NOVEMBER 26

QUESTION: Paul is praying for the early Christians, that Christ may dwell in their hearts by faith. Do you ever pray like this for your family and friends?

Ephesians 3:14-21

PRAYER SUGGESTION: Pray now for someone special to you, using Paul's words in the second paragraph.

MAY 27
NOVEMBER 27

QUESTION: It often helps our faith if we praise God in company with others. Have you ever tried it – apart from in a church service?

Psalm 34:1-7

PRAYER SUGGESTION: The Psalmist says, “I sought the Lord, and he answered me; he delivered me from all my fears.” If this is your experience, then praise him now with your lips.

* * * *

MAY 28
NOVEMBER 28

QUESTION: Do you remember Peter? Denying he ever knew Jesus? There at the resurrection? Peter now praises the early Christians who believe the claims of Jesus, without being there to see Jesus.

1 Peter 1:3-9

PRAYER: Thank you, Jesus, that though I’ve never seen you as Peter did, you have shown yourself to me in a way that allows me be filled with an inexpressible and glorious joy.

MAY 29
NOVEMBER 29

QUESTION: When hard times come, do you think God wants you to come even closer to him, or is this when you turn away from him?

John 15:1-8
Continued tomorrow

PRAYER: When things are hard and painful, then please, Lord God, help me follow you more closely.

* * * *

MAY 30
NOVEMBER 30

Continued from yesterday
QUESTION: Jesus wants us to remain in his love. Do the words of Jesus in today's reading help you to love other people, even those who are unkind to you?

John 15:9-17

PRAYER: Lord Jesus, thank you for your perfect love. Help me show this love to others.

MAY 31

QUESTION: Who are the people who are the light of the world? Not us, surely? Yes we are, so we must be careful how we behave, so that people will praise God and not us – or worse still, find fault with us.

Matthew 5:13-16

PRAYER: Lord, let my light shine before men, that they may see my good deeds and praise my Father in Heaven – and not praise me.

JUNE 1
DECEMBER 1

QUESTION: Do you try to be "righteous" by your own strength, or by the strength that comes from Jesus? Is there a difference between your own righteousness and the righteousness that comes from Jesus?

Philippians 1:3-11

PRAYER: Lord Jesus, please help me grow closer to you every day, so that I may be filled with your love and righteousness.

* * * *

JUNE 2
DECEMBER 2

QUESTION: When the psalmist says the Lord is his rock and fortress, what do you think he means?

Psalm 31:1-5

PRAYER SUGGESTION: Say the psalmist's prayer from these verses: "Into your hands I commit my spirit; redeem me, O LORD, the God of truth."

JUNE 3
DECEMBER 3

QUESTION: Do you always understand what you read in the Bible? If you don't, you're in good company, as we're going to see here.

John 20:1-9

PRAYER: Lord, so often I have heard about you, yet there are so many things I just don't understand. Please teach me, and help me to listen.

* * * *

JUNE 4
DECEMBER 4

QUESTION: In Old Testament times the people could not approach God by themselves, but needed a priest to do it for them. Why can you now approach God directly?

Hebrews 10:19-25

PRAYER: Dear God, thank you that, because Jesus died for me, I can now approach you directly. Help me approach you more often than I do.

JUNE 5
DECEMBER 5

QUESTION: Do you sometimes think you deserve a place in Heaven – or do you sometimes think you don't deserve a place? Salvation and forgiveness are a gift that no one deserves.

Ephesians 2:1-10

PRAYER: Lord God, I want to say thank you for the gift of salvation and forgiveness, because they are things I could never earn.

* * * *

JUNE 6
DECEMBER 6

QUESTION: Do you think of yourself as a citizen of Heaven? You don't have to wait. You can get citizenship immediately – just by asking.

Philippians 3:17-21

PRAYER: Thank you, Lord, that I am already a citizen of Heaven. Please help me look forward to being in Heaven with you.

JUNE 7
DECEMBER 7

QUESTION: Samuel has come to find the new King of Israel – David. How do we judge people, and how does God?

1 Samuel 16:4-7

PRAYER: I thank you, Lord, that even though you can see deep inside me, you still love me.

* * * *

JUNE 8
DECEMBER 8

QUESTION: This reading is all about God's love for us. How much do you love him? How much does he love you?

John 14:15-21

PRAYER: Father God, please help me love you even more, and please let the Holy Spirit fill my life all through the day and all through the night.

JUNE 9
DECEMBER 9

QUESTION: Where does your help come from? Is it from the place where the Psalmist gets his help?

Psalm 121:1-8

PRAYER: Lord, so many times in my life I look in the wrong place for help. Please be so close to me that I always turn to you first.

* * * *

JUNE 10
DECEMBER 10

QUESTION: Think about this one carefully. Should you put yourself last in order to be first? Or put yourself last in order to have the privilege of being the servant of all?

Mark 9:33-37

PRAYER: Help me, Lord, to be willing to serve rather than be served. Help me be willing to be the servant of all.

JUNE 11
DECEMBER 11

QUESTION: What does God look like? Paul says that Jesus is the image of God on earth. No, we can't see Jesus, but we can read about him and in this way get a clearer picture of God.

Colossians 1:15-23a

PRAYER: Lord Jesus, thank you that in you we can see God. Help me "continue in my faith, established and firm, and not moved from the hope held out in the gospel."

* * * *

JUNE 12
DECEMBER 12

QUESTION: Are you, like Nicodemus, puzzled when you hear about people being "born again"? What do you think the expression means?

John 3:1-8
Continued tomorrow

PRAYER: Jesus, you taught that we have to be born again. Don't let me be like Nicodemus, help me understand the mystery even more than I do now.

JUNE 13
DECEMBER 13

Continued from yesterday
QUESTION: How much does God love the world? Why does this mean we need never perish?

John 3:9-18

PRAYER: Heavenly Father, thank you for not just loving the world, but for loving me as well.

* * * *

JUNE 14
DECEMBER 14

QUESTION: What does it mean, as Paul says here, to do everything in the name of the Lord Jesus? Are you doing it already?

Colossians 3:12-17

PRAYER: Thank you, Lord, for everything you've done for me. Please let the peace of Christ rule in my heart.

JUNE 15
DECEMBER 15

QUESTION: Have you "tasted the Lord"? You have? Have you found him good?

Psalm 34:8-14

PRAYER: Lord, please help me trust you, and take refuge safely in you.

* * * *

JUNE 16
DECEMBER 16

QUESTION: Have you wondered what Jesus is doing at this moment? Clue: Read the third paragraph here. Isn't that amazing?

Romans 8:31b-39

PRAYER: Thank you, Jesus, that even now you are at the right hand of God the Father, interceding for me. Help me see that whatever happens, nothing can separate me from the love of God.

JUNE 17
DECEMBER 17

QUESTION: In the Old Testament a perfect lamb had to sacrificed, in order to remove sin. But who is the perfect Lamb of God mentioned here?

Revelation 5:8-13

PRAYER SUGGESTION: Try saying these words from this reading – and mean them. “Worthy is the Lamb, who was slain, to receive power and wealth and wisdom and strength and honour and glory and praise!”

* * * *

JUNE 18
DECEMBER 18

QUESTION: Do you sometimes think you’re not good enough to be a Christian? Paul says he has the same trouble, but he knows that Jesus is patient with him.

1 Timothy 1:15-17

PRAYER: Lord Jesus, I cannot thank you enough that you’re patient with me, in spite of all my failings. Please help me trust you more.

JUNE 19
DECEMBER 19

QUESTION: Do you sometimes wonder where God is? If you do, you're in good company! See what the Psalmist says.

Psalm 42:1-6a

PRAYER SUGGESTION: The Psalmist says, "Put your hope in God, for I will yet praise him, my Saviour and my God." Try it!

SPECIAL READINGS FOR CHRISTMAS

(GO TO PAGE 95 FOR JUNE READINGS)

DECEMBER 20

QUESTION: We can often take this story for granted, because we know it so well. Mary hadn't heard it before. How do you think she felt?

Luke 1:26-33

PRAYER: Thank you, Heavenly Father, that you chose Mary to be the mother of the Saviour of the world. Thank you for her faithfulness to you.

* * * *

DECEMBER 21

QUESTION: This is such a familiar story that you may have stopped looking in it for anything special. How about looking at the meaning of the name Immanuel? What exactly does it mean, and why is it the name of Jesus?

Matthew 1:18-24

PRAYER: Thank you, Jesus, that when you were born as a baby on earth, God came to us. May this Christmas be a special one, when I learn new things about you.

DECEMBER 22

QUESTION: Mary was "greatly troubled" by the news the angel had brought about having a baby. What do you think Joseph thought about it?

Luke 2:1-7

PRAYER: Heavenly Father, thank you that Mary and Joseph were faithful to you. Life must have been hard for them, especially during the birth of our Saviour. Help me go through difficult times willingly for you.

* * * *

DECEMBER 23

QUESTION: Do you think today's reading was written a year before Jesus was born, ten years, a hundred years or seven hundred years? Clue: Think big!

Isaiah 9:6-7

PRAYER: How amazing, Lord God, that the birth of our Saviour was foretold by Isaiah so many years ago, and that you planned the coming of Jesus even before creation.

DECEMBER 24

QUESTION: Imagine you're out on the hills with the shepherds. How are you going to react when the angels suddenly appear?

Luke 2:8-14

PRAYER SUGGESTION: Give glory to God, along with the angels.

* * * *

DECEMBER 25 – CHRISTMAS DAY

QUESTION: Can you remember when you first heard about Jesus? How long did it take for you to hurry off and find him?

Luke 2:15-20

PRAYER: Thank you, Jesus, that I've found you for myself. I may not have hurried to find you as fast as the shepherds did, so I thank you now for your patience in waiting for me.

(Go to Page 98 for December 26)

JUNE 20

QUESTION: If you've started building your house on sand, have you left it too late to do anything about it? Clue: Jesus can rebuild your life for you, on his own strong foundation.

Matthew 7:24-29

PRAYER: Help me, Jesus, to have you as a strong foundation in my life, so that when the storms come I will be safe for ever.

* * * *

JUNE 21

QUESTION: Who brought the good news to the people, that God reigns? Who brings it today?

Isaiah 52:7-11

PRAYER: Thank you, Lord, for the prophets in the Old Testament who brought Good News to the people, for the apostles and other workers who spread the Good News of Jesus from country to country, and for the workers today who preach so faithfully.

JUNE 22

QUESTION: How do you find your way through life? By trial and error – or by walking with Jesus?

John 8:12-19

PRAYER: Heavenly Father, thank you for sending Jesus. Help me see the light that your Son shines on the way, so that I may walk on it safely – with him.

* * * *

JUNE 23

QUESTION: Has God come to you and made his home with you yet? He will. This is a promise from Jesus.

John 14:22-27

PRAYER: Please, Lord God, make your home with me, and help me love and obey you.

JUNE 24

QUESTION: Do you think this reading is the cry of a desperate person, or a shout of praise for God's faithfulness?

Psalm 3:1-7

PRAYER SUGGESTION: Think of your present troubles, and consider God's goodness and faithfulness. Try and get them both into perspective, and talk with God about your conclusion.

* * * *

JUNE 25

QUESTION: When you're in need, do you think Jesus' heart goes out to you, or do you think he shrugs and turns the other way? Don't always think the answers to your prayers will be in the way you expect.

Luke 7:11-17

PRAYER: Jesus, help me know and feel your great love and compassion for me in times of great need. Even if my prayers aren't answered in the way I ask, let me know that you are in charge, and that your heart goes out to me.

JUNE 26
DECEMBER 26

QUESTION: Do you sometimes want to shout aloud in praise of God? Try it sometime. And try bowing down today in worship. These are good things to do when you can.

Psalm 95:1-7a

PRAYER: Forgive me, Lord, for the times when I have just taken you for granted, and not offered you thanksgiving and praise. (Maybe you could try doing something about it now.)

* * * *

JUNE 27
DECEMBER 27

QUESTION: How long will God love us for? Six months, a few years – or for ever?

Psalm 107:1-9

PRAYER SUGGESTION FROM TODAY'S READING: "Give thanks to the LORD, for he is good; his love endures for ever."

JUNE 28
DECEMBER 28

QUESTION: This reading is so amazing that it's easy to miss the point. If we are children of God, and Jesus is the Son of God, does that make Jesus your brother? Read the passage. Can you now think of Jesus in a different light – he's your big, caring brother, as well as your Saviour!

Mark 3:31-35

PRAYER: Jesus, thank you that we are your brothers and sisters. And thank you too that you are my brother.

* * * *

JUNE 29
DECEMBER 29

QUESTION: One day Jesus will come back – in a spectacular way that everyone will see. Are you looking forward to that time? You should be!

1 Thessalonians 4:13-18

PRAYER: Lord Jesus, help me look forward with excitement to the time when you will come back and take me to Heaven.

JUNE 30
DECEMBER 30

QUESTION: Jesus can meet every need. Here he heals the sick. But Jesus asks one man if he wants to get well! Why? Do we really want our prayers answered in the way we ask, or can we trust Jesus to give us what is best?

John 5:1b-9a

PRAYER: Lord Jesus, I don't want to tell you what to do, but you know my needs. I ask that you will answer my prayers in the way that you think best. Help me trust you in this.

* * * *

DECEMBER 31

QUESTION: How much do you love Jesus? Remember, the more he's forgiven you, the more you'll love him. Maybe that's why some people love him more than others.

Luke 7:41-50

PRAYER: Lord Jesus, help me realize just how much you have forgiven me, so that I may love you more and more.

EASTER

SPECIAL EASTER READINGS, STARTING HERE ON PALM SUNDAY – THE SUNDAY BEFORE EASTER

PALM SUNDAY

QUESTION: What a wonderful sight it must have been to see the crowd praising and welcoming Jesus. Look at the last line of the reading. Where have you heard words like these before? Clue: Shepherds in December.

Luke 19:28b-38

PRAYER SUGGESTION: Use your own words to praise and welcome Jesus.

MONDAY BEFORE EASTER

QUESTION: Where is Jesus now? Still on the cross, or seated at the right hand of the mighty God?

Luke 22:66-71

PRAYER: Thank you, Jesus, that you died and rose again, and are now at the right hand of the mighty God.

* * * *

TUESDAY BEFORE EASTER

QUESTION: Do you think the disciples understood what Jesus was saying here, at the Last Supper? What was Jesus telling them?

Luke 22:14-20

PRAYER: Jesus, please help me understand what it means that your body was given for me, and your blood was shed for me.

WEDNESDAY BEFORE EASTER

QUESTION: Jesus could have saved his life by giving the "right" answers to the high priest's questions – especially as it might have saved his life. What did Jesus mean about destroying and rebuilding the temple in three days?

Mark 14:55-62

PRAYER: Lord, it's often easier to take the simple way out in life when asked about my faith in you. Help me have the confidence to talk about you openly and boldly.

* * * *

THURSDAY BEFORE EASTER

QUESTION: This is another prophecy from Isaiah, written 700 years before the time of Jesus. How have people gone astray? Clue: Jesus used the same picture language.

Isaiah 53:3-6

PRAYER: Lord, like a sheep I have indeed gone astray, but you found me and brought me safely home. Thank you for keeping me safely in your hand.

GOOD FRIDAY (TWO READINGS FOR TODAY)

QUESTION: This is an account of a terrible and cruel event. So why is it in this book? Clue: Think about what would have happened to you if the Lamb of God had avoided the crucifixion and died of old age!

Matthew 27:27-31

PRAYER: Lord Jesus, help me understand just how awful this must have been for you, and I want to thank you that you did it for me.

* * * *

GOOD FRIDAY (SECOND READING FOR TODAY)

QUESTION: Jesus is on the cross. Two criminals being crucified with Jesus ask him to save them. But does one of them mean it? Why is only one criminal kept safe for eternity?

Luke 23:35-43

PRAYER SUGGESTION: Have you asked Jesus to remember you when he comes into his kingdom? If you have, thank him now. If not, ask him.

EASTER SATURDAY

QUESTION: Was Jesus really dead? Death, when nailed to a cross was violent, and Roman centurions didn't make mistakes about things like that.

Mark 15:42-47

PRAYER: Lord Jesus, thank you for the boldness of Joseph of Arimathea in identifying himself openly as a friend of yours. Help me be just as bold when I'm talking about you.

* * * *

EASTER DAY (TWO READINGS FOR TODAY)

QUESTION: Do you worship a dead Christ – or a living Christ?

Luke 24:1-8

PRAYER: Thank you, Jesus, that you're alive and here with me now. Please may I feel more and more of your presence and love day by day.

EASTER DAY (SECOND READING FOR TODAY)

QUESTION: These three women believed Jesus to be still dead. Can you imagine the shock and surprise they must have had when they got to the tomb?

Mark 16:1-7

PRAYER: Lord Jesus, my Saviour, you really did rise from the dead on Easter Day. This is wonderful news, and I want to thank you once again that you're alive today – and here with me now.

* * * *

EASTER MONDAY

QUESTION: Jesus is telling his disciples that there is much about him in the Old Testament. That makes the Old Testament important, doesn't it?

Luke 24:36-45

PRAYER: Jesus, open my eyes so that I can read about you in the Old Testament as well as the New.

TUESDAY AFTER EASTER

QUESTION: Yes, it's true: the Lord has risen from the dead! Do you sometimes forget?

Luke 24:28-35

PRAYER: Lord Jesus, there are times when I forget you are not only risen, but are here with me now. Help me remember this, so that I need no longer be anxious.

* * * *

WEDNESDAY AFTER EASTER

QUESTION: Why were the women bewildered? Hadn't Jesus told them what was going to happen? Do you sometimes get the wrong ideas about Jesus?

Matthew 28:1-10

PRAYER: As I read the Bible, Lord, make it clearer to me, so that I can know you even better.

About the Author

Chris Wright is married with three grownup children, and lives in the West Country of England where he is a home group leader with his local church. He has written many books, mostly for young readers. His Christian books currently in print with White Tree Publishing are:

Chris's books for family reading:

Mary Jones and Her Bible: An Adventure Book Paperback ISBN 978-0-9525-9562-5

Pilgrim's Progress: An Adventure Book Paperback ISBN 978-0-9525-9566-3

Pilgrim's Progress — Special Edition Paperback ISBN 978-0-9525-9567-0, e-Book ISBN: 978-0-9932760-8-8

Zephan and the Vision Paperback ISBN 978-0-9525-9569-4, e-Book ISBN: 978-0-9932760-6-4

Agathos, The Rocky Island, and Other Stories — Paperback ISBN 978-0-9525-9568-7, e-Book ISBN: 978-0-9927642-7-2

Four short books

Help! Paperback ISBN 978-0-9927642-2-7, e-Book ISBN: 978-0-9933941-1-9

So, What Is a Christian? An introduction to a personal faith. Paperback ISBN: 978-0-9927642-2-7, e-Book ISBN: 978-0-9933941-2-6

Starting Out – help for new Christians of all ages. Paperback ISBN 978-1-4839-622-0-7, e-Book ISBN: 978-0-9933941-0-2

Running Through the Bible – a simple understanding of what's in the Bible — Paperback ISBN: 978-0-9927642-6-5, e-Book ISBN: 978-0-9933941-3-3

For older readers:

English Hexapla — The Gospel of John. Paperback ISBN 978-0-9525-9561-8

Many adults enjoy ***Pilgrim's Progress — Special Edition.*** (See books above for ISBNs.) The story sticks closely to the events in John Bunyan's book and is set in that period, but Christian and Christiana are teenagers. A painless way to become familiar with the original!

You can find further details of all these books on the websites of major internet booksellers and e-Book sellers, and buy some paperback titles from bookstores. Enter *White Tree Publishing* in the relevant search box on the websites of internet book sellers to see the whole range of books. Titles are available in paperback and/or e-Book format.

Churches and Christian organizations worldwide can purchase multiple print copies of *Starting Out*, *Help!*, *So, What Is a Christian?* and *Running Through the Bible* directly from the publisher (wtpbristol@gmail.com).

WHITE
TREE
PUBLISHING

Printed in Great Britain
by Amazon

41701302R00066